'Telling' and Talking about Donor Conception with 8 – 11 yea

Contents

Telling and Talking 8 - 11 — 1

Introduction — 1

Deciding to Tell — 2
- What others have to say about 'telling' — 2
- Overcoming your fears can only benefit the family — 3
- Anxiety about 'telling' is normal — 4

Preparing to Tell — 4
- Parents and 'telling' — 5
- Talking with others as part of preparing to tell — 6

Language — 6

Your child's development — 7
- Children's development and being a 'real' parent — 7
- Dealing with the Dad question — 9
- Ages eight and nine — 9
- Ages 10 and 11 — 10

Telling for the first time — 12
- Non-genetic parents and 'telling' — 14
- Genetic parents and 'telling' — 14
- Doing the 'telling' alone when you started parenting as a couple — 14

Telling and Talking if you have a known donor — 15

Identifiable or anonymous donor — 18
- Going abroad and the 'telling' question — 19
- Lessons from adoption — 19
- Telling and talking when you have an anonymous donor — 19

First and on-going reactions to being 'Told' — 20
- Who am I? — 20
- Issues about resemblance — 21
- Siblings — 22
- Dealing with difference — 22
- Making genetic connections. Questions about the donor and half-siblings — 23

Talking with others — 24
- Family and friends — 24
- School matters — 26

Final thoughts — 29
- Offical support for 'telling' — 29
- Mixed feelings are OK — 30
- Remember that children develop in different ways — 30
- Final words from parents — 31

Further Reading — 32

Films — 33

Useful Contacts — 35

Acknowledgements and thanks

These materials would not have been produced without the financial backing of the Parenting Fund. This Government funding, administered through the National Family and Parenting Institute, is competitively provided for the voluntary and community sector in England to strengthen support services for parents. Very many thanks are due to those who took a chance and backed an unusual way of supporting parents.

I am enormously grateful to: Ken Daniels, Professor (Adjunct) of Social Work at the University of Canterbury, New Zealand; Marilyn Crawshaw, Lecturer in Social Work and Research Fellow at the University of York; and Jennie Hunt, Senior Counsellor at the Wolfson Family Clinic, Hammersmith Hospital, London, who painstakingly read and thoughtfully considered all four booklets. Their wisdom, knowledge and long experience of donor conception issues have immeasurably improved both the content and the way it is expressed.

The sections on child development have benefited greatly from Elizabeth Howell's depth of knowledge and experience of working with parents and children.

Janice Stevens Botsford, a donor conceived adult who has found some of her genetic siblings and discovered the identity of her donor, brought her compassion, thoughtfulness and passion for the truth to the booklet for parents of those aged 17 and over.

Marion Scott, Steering Group member of DC Network and mentor to How to Tell, made sure that the project kept on-track and provided invaluable support when I was flagging.

Sarah Gillam suggested the structure for the booklets and has edited and re-edited the texts with much patience.

Nothing would have been possible without the many families and individuals inside and outside DC Network who have talked with me in person, on the 'phone and by email about their thoughts, feelings and experiences of donor conception. It has been a privilege to hear your stories. Thank you for your permission to share them.

Lastly, but definitely not least, my thanks to my family, Walter, Dan, Will and 'Zannah. Your love, patience and support has kept me going.

Olivia Montuschi
April 2006

Telling and Talking
8 – 11

"Having not been sure for a while of exactly how much my eldest child understood about her origins, we had the most amazing discussion yesterday prompted by a school session on the subject of periods!"
Mother of 10 year old girl.

Introduction

This booklet is for all parents of 8 to 11 year olds who have built their families with the help of donor conception (sperm, eggs or embryos). It is likely that one of the two scenarios below describes your situation –

- you have not yet told your child or children about their origins, but you are now seriously thinking about it or have already decided that you are going to share information with them about how they came to be part of the family

or

- you began the process of 'telling' your child or children at an earlier age but are looking for information related to this stage of their development as a support to continuing the conversation.

The aim of this booklet is to support you with feeling comfortable with the idea of 'telling' and to give you practical help in starting and continuing that process. What it does not do is prescribe a single 'right way' of going about 'telling', because all parents and children are different and you will find your own ways of starting and continuing to share the story of how your family was made.

Over the next few pages you will find acknowledgement of some of the hopes and fears that are often present when talking about this subject, some very practical suggestions about how you can prepare yourself for such conversations, and some insight into the potential feelings and responses of your child or children. There is also guidance on setting the scene when 'telling' for the first time.

For both first time and continuing tellers, you will find information about what is likely to be happening developmentally for your child or children at this stage of their lives, and how they may react or respond to donor conception issues at home and at school. Throughout the booklet you will find quotes from professionals, donor conceived young people and their parents.

If you are thinking of starting to 'tell' at this stage then it is probable that you are part of a heterosexual couple and this is the assumption that has been made throughout this booklet. Single women and same sex couples are likely to have already responded to some of their children's questions about fathers or mothers by this age. Couples, heterosexual or gay, needing to use a surrogate to carry a child sometimes require donor eggs, so need to be able to explain that part of their child's creation as well as the fact of surrogacy. However, if

'Telling' and Talking about Donor Conception with 8 – 11 year olds

you are reading this to get help with continuing the conversation with your child or children, then most of the information here is appropriate for same sex couples and solo mums as well.

Although infertility is the reason that most heterosexual couples need to use donor conception, some people will have done so in order to avoid passing on a genetic condition. The vast majority of this leaflet is relevant for both situations.

Deciding to Tell

Coming to this decision may or may not have been difficult, although it would be unusual if you didn't have some mixed feelings about the actual 'telling'. You may have always planned to tell at this age, believing that your child would be old enough to understand by this time. Or it could be that you had planned to tell earlier but the right opportunity didn't seem to occur and time just slipped away. Alternatively you might have originally decided to keep the secret, but have changed your mind since then.

There has been a considerable change in the way of thinking about 'telling' over the last few years. The Human Fertilisation and Embryology Authority (HFEA) now requires clinics to encourage and prepare couples and individuals undergoing donor conception treatment to tell their children about their origins from an early age.

For some parents the decision to be open is clear and untroubled from the start. The only questions are when and how to do it. For others the decision is not so clear. They may be full of apprehension about what would happen (to both themselves and their children) if they did tell. Sometimes couples find that although they both agreed to donor conception, they disagree on the issue of 'telling'. Because sperm, egg or embryo donation for heterosexual couples is usually invisible to the outside world, there is a temptation to believe that 'telling' may not be important.

"After all, she's our child, we're going to love her to bits, so why does she need to know?"

Another group of parents believe that 'telling' is probably the right thing to do, but emotionally don't feel ready or don't know where to begin, so put off starting the process. As time passes it becomes more and more difficult to begin.

By contrast, solo mums and same sex parents are often faced with the question, "Have I got a dad/mum?" from when their child is about two, so 'telling' is something they are likely to have started well before their child has reached the age of eight.

What others have to say about 'telling'

Professionals like Ken Daniels, a social work professor, and Diane Ehrensaft, a clinical psychologist, believe that families fare better if the information about how that family came into being is known by all members. It is now increasingly realised that it can be unhealthy for family relationships to keep such significant information a secret, partly because of the energy that is taken up by doing so and the pressure this creates for parents. As children grow older and become more curious about the world in general and family connections in particular, parents may find themselves avoiding subjects around family likenesses or even directly lying. And there is always the worry that they might find out from someone else. Many donor conceived teenagers and adults who have found out that they were conceived in this way have made it clear that they believe they should have grown up with this information from very early in their lives.

There remains a gap, however, between what professionals now believe is right – and indeed the philosophy on which DC Network is based – and the feelings of many parents who remain full of fears and anxieties about telling. These fears are understandable and many of them will be addressed later in this booklet, but they are not themselves reasons to keep donor conception secret. The following list is adapted from one first drawn up by Diane Ehrensaft. It gives what she feels are the only three good reasons for not telling children at all or postponing telling to a different time. All of them put the best interests of children first –

1. Issues to do with the child's ability to understand: children with significant learning or developmental problems may well not be able to take in information about their origins.

2. Issues for the bond between parent and child: for instance, if a parent has been away from a child for a long time for any reason, re-building this relationship should come before 'telling'. Where parents are separating or divorcing, 'telling' should never be used as a threat to break a relationship between parent and child. Unless children are at real risk of learning about their origins from someone other than a parent, telling should ideally only begin when both parents agree and the emotional climate has settled down.

3. Issues for the child from outside the immediate family: if wider family members or those in the community are likely to reject a child conceived by donated sperm, eggs or embryos, then it is difficult for a child to feel any sense of pride about their origins. This can apply where a child is being brought up within a culture or faith that disapproves of donor conception.

Ehrensaft goes on to point out that parents need to be very honest with themselves. Concerns that a child may be upset or confused by being 'told' can cover anxieties and fears that properly belong to the parent and are not really to do with the child at all.

Overcoming your fears can only benefit the family

This is the heart of the matter. As adults we think and feel about donor conception (and everything else) through the filter of our own experiences and perceptions. As parents we want to protect our children from the worst elements of our own experiences and the prejudices of others. Our children, however, do not share our history, so they have no assumptions about what being donor conceived might mean. They are starting out in life and deserve

'Telling' and Talking about Donor Conception with 8 – 11 year olds

the opportunity to be proud of who they are. Donor conception is a non-traditional way for a child to come into a family. It is different, but difference doesn't have to be bad, it is just…different. How we respond to difference of any kind depends on our upbringing, personality and experiences. Children can be helped to be proud of their difference or they can learn to hide it… or be aware of something being hidden from them. Many donor conceived adults who have found out about their beginnings say that they had felt that something was odd or wrong in their family long before they were 'told'.

Putting aside deeply held fears and anxieties, even to benefit our children, may not be easy at first, but Network parents who have taken the plunge report feeling greatly relieved once they have had the first conversation.

Geoff contacted DC Network for advice about telling his 11 year old son Andrew about his beginnings by sperm donation. He wrote later:

> "Angela and I have told Andrew about his donor father, after we read the books you sent us. It has gone incredibly well! We are a very happy and relieved mum and dad. It does not seem to have changed things for us as a family. He went a bit insecure, but my dad died two weeks ago and at first Andrew thought it made a difference to his grandad not being a proper grandad. He has now thought it through and decided he was his grandad after all, so all is OK. I would like to say thank you so much for your listening and advice to an anxious dad who wanted to do the right thing and not alienate his beloved boy."

Anxiety about 'telling' is normal

Very few parents have no anxieties at all about the actual 'how to' of telling. Even those most committed to openness sometimes get sick feelings in the pit of their stomach before they start to talk with their child.

Your confidence that telling is the right thing to do and comfort with the decisions you have made are the keys to your children being able to feel the same way. Good preparation – detailed below – is the key to you feeling comfortable. That said, children are mostly pretty resilient, so don't feel you have to get it right all of the time.

Preparing to Tell

Telling a child in this age group for the first time is different from beginning to share information with younger children. Instead of building up small pieces of information over the years, you will need to explain simply but clearly exactly how and why they came to be conceived with donated eggs, sperm or embryos. You will also need to be ready to talk about sex and unassisted reproduction as well. Some books to help with this are listed at the end of this booklet. Although the story books for children (published by DC Network and others) to help share donor conception information with children are aimed at under sevens, they can still be a useful introduction for this age group. There is something about the very simple language that makes it easy for a child to take in the information offered. They also provide a good example for parents in keeping language straightforward. Reading our book Archie Nolan: Family Detective, which is intended for this age group, BEFORE your child, may help you understand the range of questions your child might ask and give ideas about ways in which you could respond. Also available are some excellent books aimed at parents that detail the experiences of families. Practising some of the language with your partner (if you have one) or with wider family and friends or a counsellor is also very helpful. But the three things that may help most are –

- giving yourself time to think about what 'telling' means for you and how you feel now about your infertility (or situation or other condition that led you to use donor conception), and your decision to build your family this way
- building up your confidence in the ways suggested in this booklet
- knowing something about the stage of development that your child is at so that you are aware of what they are likely to understand and how they may respond to information about donor conception.

Parents and 'telling'

In order for a whole family to benefit most from openness about donor conception, parents need to feel that not only are they doing the right thing for their children but that they can also (now or in the future) feel good themselves about having created their family in this way. This comes easily for some but for others it can take time. It may involve taking some risks and perhaps at times acting with greater outer confidence than is felt on the inside for a while. One of the things that can get in the way is if there are any deep seated unresolved feelings about infertility or the need to use the sperm or egg from someone other than a loved partner to conceive a child.

Donor conception for family creation is not the first choice of any heterosexual couple, or most single women. Same sex couples also have many questions to face before going ahead. This method of conception almost always follows considerable heartache over a long period of time. There is a need to grieve the loss of a longed-for biological child of your relationship or, for many single women, loss of the hope of having a child as part of a loving couple. This is a significant part of the process that leads to the eventual decision to pursue other ways of becoming a parent or adjusting to childlessness. It takes time to grieve for the child you cannot have. It may be that such grieving has to happen before it is possible to make the necessary adjustments and really welcome the child you can have. Although this grieving process ideally takes place before a child is conceived, sometimes it doesn't work out that way. It may be that once on the roller-coaster of fertility treatment it felt difficult to break the cycle of investigations and treatments in order to raise the question of whether you felt ready to have a child using a donor. Sometimes men or women put pressure on their partner to agree to go ahead, and sometimes partners go along with what they think the other one wants, without really feeling ready themselves. It can be the persistence of feelings about such issues that has got in the way of not 'telling' a child about donor conception earlier. It is never too late to re-visit some of these feelings.

'Telling' and Talking about Donor Conception with 8 – 11 year olds

Putting aside time now to talk about, recognise and acknowledge the losses that you have gone through and any feelings of shame or stigma that may still be around, can be some of the most helpful preparation you are likely to do for 'telling'. You may choose to talk with your partner, a close family member or friend, someone from DC Network or to see a counsellor, either returning to your clinic or seeking someone new.

Taking what feels like a risk and talking with others about difficult thoughts and feelings often plays an important part in parents realising that 'telling' is not so terrible or difficult after all. DC Network meetings have proved this time and again. One mum and dad to a daughter age eight, put it this way –

> "We were so afraid of telling her…we seemed to freeze up inside every time something came up, like her talking about who she looked like. She must have felt there was something wrong…we just changed the subject or looked the other way. Coming to Network meetings gave us so much confidence and last time we just went straight home and 'told' her. She didn't bat an eyelid, but we've all felt much closer as a family since then."

A sense of feeling closer as a family is often reported by parents following 'telling'. This seems to be to do with relieving the anxiety of keeping the secret and removing what felt like a barrier to honest relationships in the family.

Talking with others as part of preparing to tell

The information you are preparing to 'tell' will belong to your child. If they are eight or nine then you may want to decide together who else should know. At 10 or 11 the information is theirs to share as they choose, but they may welcome some support and guidance around who else might need to know. You may feel, however, that it would be helpful to prepare the ground first by telling other significant family members, such as your own parents. There may be people within the family or wider family or friendship networks, whom your child may turn to for support, so consider letting them know what you are planning to do. Involving someone such as a godparent or special friend, who has the interests of your child at heart but is not immediately emotionally involved, may be very helpful. There is a difference between others having known for a long time whilst your child remained unknowing, and sharing the information immediately before 'telling' in order to provide a network of support.

Taking your time to think about these issues, and talking with each other, a trusted friend, family member or a counsellor BEFORE you talk with your child or children is really important: the better prepared you are, the more confident you will feel and the more confident you are feeling, the more secure your child is likely to feel.

Language

Throughout this booklet the term 'donor' is used to refer to the person whose gift enabled the building of a family. Using the word 'father' or 'mother' by itself or 'real mother or father' can confuse the role of donor with that of the person who is, on a daily basis, fathering or mothering a child. The donor does have an undeniable genetic connection to the children he or she helped create and deserves to be referred to with respect and gratitude, but identifiable at 18 or anonymous donors do not have a parenting role and are not part of the family. Different language may develop where there is a known donor or co-parenting situation (see section on Known Donors).

Small children usually take on the language used by their parents, but from around the age of eight, they may go through times of using different words. Experience has shown that the word children use for their donor often, but not always, changes with their stage of development and rarely has anything to do with the quality of relationships within a family. It is simply evidence that a child (probably without knowing it) is working things out for themselves.

> Sophie age 10, conceived with a donated embryo, has recently shown that she is beginning to understand about the lack of genetic connection to either of her parents by saying, when talking about her donors, "So technically they are my mum and dad". Her mum Stephanie's first feeling was to become defensive and deny this but she resisted the urge and instead talked calmly with Sophie about what this might mean.

See the next section on Your child's development for more about language.

Your child's development

Children's development takes place on three main fronts –
- physical growth that is completed by late teens and early twenties
- cognitive (thinking and learning) growth, which is at its height in babyhood, childhood and early teenage years
- emotional and social growth, the foundations of which are laid in early years and are then built on throughout life.

Each child develops at his or her own rate and as it is rare for all three areas of development to take place at the same time the different growing processes are often out of sync with each other. One child may have a growth spurt that leaves them looking much more mature than they are emotionally, whilst another can remain small and child-like in appearance at the same time as being advanced intellectually and socially.

Physical growth continues unless it is inhibited by something dramatic such as lack of food. Cognitive, social and emotional development occur as the result of experiences. These experiences influence the unseen development of the brain.

Children's development and being a 'real' parent

At around the age of eight children usually make a leap in brain development that often shows itself in increased understanding of the world around them and an ability to manage themselves and life generally in ever more independent and competent ways. They are likely to be able to understand more in depth information about donor conception and genetic connections. Sex and relationship education from parents and at school adds to this knowledge. However, the thinking capacity, particularly of pre-teen boys, tends to be pretty uncomplicated and literal. Following from this, they often think that if they have inherited genes from their donor then he or she must be their 'real' father or mother. The use of the word 'real' seems to be unconnected to the emotional relationship they have with the person who loves and cares for them day to day and whom they would not dream of rejecting in favour of their donor. It is used because no other word fits the rational and conventional linking of genes and family relationships. This may change as they mature and eventually take on the more complex thinking that is characteristic of the second half of the teenage years.

Some parents, particularly those who are not genetically related to a child, can be very sensitive about challenges to their status and authority as a 'real' parent. The phrase that seems to haunt some parents starts, "You're not my real mother/father, you can't tell me what to do." Despite the experience in DC Network that only a minority of children and young people do confront their mother or father in this way, something along these lines certainly does happen in *some* families and often earlier than teenage years. Sometimes it is because the frustration and anger of a particular moment leads a child to use whatever weapon comes to hand to try to hurt a parent. At other times, particularly at this stage, it can be as a response to sadness at the recent realisation that a much loved parent is not genetically connected to them. John, a Network member, related this story in an edition of DC Network News.

> "One night, about three years ago, I was reading Ben (age eight) a bedtime story. I was tired and after I had got through two short chapters (perhaps in a rather hurried way), I shut the book decisively. He pleaded with me to carry on. I refused, said goodnight to him and walked out of the room. He shouted after me, 'You're not my father anyway.'
> I went back to him, 'Oh no,' I said, 'Who is then?'
> I don't know,' he muttered, 'somebody else, somewhere else.'
> 'OK,' I said and walked out again.
> He immediately called me back, 'I'm sorry Daddy,' he said, 'I wish you were my sperm father.'
> I told him that it didn't matter, hugged him and went downstairs."

Understanding that such a challenge is not a personal attack on you, but has come about as a result of your child having absorbed the information you have been telling them, may help you respond in ways that are neither tearful nor defensive. Recognising and acknowledging your child's feelings is always helpful.

> Tom, age 9, is one of twins conceived by embryo donation to solo mum Lucia. Whilst seeing their GP recently for a matter unrelated to donor conception, Tom said to Lucia, "So if the seed came from a man and the egg came from another lady, does that mean you're not my real mummy?" Lucia did not answer directly but suggested to Tom that he have a think about that question and that they would talk about it later. In the car as they were going home he said, "I have thought about it and I think you ARE my real mum".

'Telling' and Talking about Donor Conception with 8 – 11 year olds

> "Max age 11 was conceived with the help of a known egg donor in Belgium. His parents had started telling him about his beginnings around age 5 but he showed little interest. After this he asked his mother Ann from time to time, "Mama, who are you?" He had a special intonation in his voice when he said this and Ann knew what he was going to say when she heard it. Ann always told him she was his mother and loved him very much. At age 8 he placed more emphasis on this question, saying, "Mama, who really, really are you?" Ann then explained fully about the egg donation and this time he understood and was very receptive to hearing about it. He wondered if he could have any brothers or sisters in his classroom."

See the booklet for parents of 12 – 16 year olds for further discussion about the use of the word 'real' with regard to parents.

Dealing with the Dad question

Solo mums and lesbian couples are likely to have been answering their children's questions about whether or not they have a dad and where he might be from as early as age two. Although most children by age eight will have understood that a man was involved in helping to create them but that they do not have a dad in their family, this does not mean that some children give up wanting to have a daddy. This seems to be particularly true for some, although definitely not all, solo mum families.

> "Solo mum Lucia knows that her 9 year old twins Tom and Amelia want a daddy very badly. They ask Lucia if she is too old to get married and they fantasise wistfully about a daddy who will mess about with them and bring a puppy into their lives. The twins are loved and cared for regularly by Lucia's brother but they still feel they would like a daddy."
>
> Lucia used to feel guilty about deliberately having had her children without a father (although she would have loved to have had a partner with whom to have a family) but now feels that this is unhelpful for the children who need her to be more matter of fact, whilst remaining a caring and always listening mum. She reckons that only about 5 to 10 per cent of her children's time is taken up with donor conception or 'daddy' talk. Most of the time they are just ordinary nine year old children.

Ages eight and nine

If life is going well generally for an individual child and their family, then eight and nine can be a truly delightful stage. Although often wishing to be with friends of a similar age, they are still usually happy to take part in family outings and can be excellent companions, being thoughtful, eager to learn and full of enthusiasm for most suggested activities. On the other hand they are also more likely to notice (and point out loudly) any differences between what you do and what you say, and perhaps be quite judgemental about habits, like smoking, that they have learned at school are not good for people's health. This is an excellent time to consolidate parent-child relationships before the potentially more rocky period of pre-adolescence starts.

'Telling' and Talking about Donor Conception with 8 – 11 year olds

For families where the 'telling' process started much earlier, this may be the moment when the penny drops. Children begin to put together all the information that has been given gradually over the years and understand that donor conception means that they are not linked biologically to one or other or perhaps both parents. This may or may not lead to a sudden spate of questions or, as in the example quoted above, some sadness at the realisation that a much loved parent is not genetically connected to them. The news, however, is not a shock because of the slow build up of information from when they were little. Children of this age are typically pretty open and unselfconscious and if donor conception has comfortably been on the family agenda for some time they are likely to feel OK about asking questions that are important to them.

> But parents can sometimes read too much into what their children are saying and Rachel, who has three children by egg donation, found herself in this situation one day when her daughter Imogen age eight said to her, "Why can't you be a proper mother to me?" Immediately fearing rejection and with her heart leaping into her mouth, Rachel enquired what she meant. Her daughter responded crossly, "Why can't you be more sensible!"

This is an age when you need to be ready to discuss anything about donor conception as well as about sex and non-assisted reproduction. It may be helpful to practice with your partner (if you have one) or with close family or friends some of the language you may want to use. If you are ready for this stage and feeling secure and confident with openness and in your parenting, then you are likely to convey this ease when talking with your children.

One Network dad decided to give a straightforward answer to his son when he asked about how sperm was donated –

> "One Friday night as we were driving to the local chip shop my eight year old son suddenly said, 'Daddy, how do you donate sperm?' I thought it was a reasonable question so I told him. 'Euugh!' he said. After this it was hard to persuade him that for adult men this strange activity was more usually associated with a rather personal kind of enjoyment, for I tried to explain this as well. After all it's not a clinical procedure."

If you are 'telling' for the first time at this age then the guidelines for setting the scene and language to use in the section on Telling are likely to be helpful. Starting to tell the story before puberty starts may well mean that any initial shock or surprise can be overcome relatively easily. Again, good preparation, your confidence and comfort and willingness to talk whenever they need to, will be the key to your child being able to feel the same way.

Ages 10 and 11

In the final primary school year many girls make a leap in physical and social development that leaves their male counterparts looking like little boys next to them. Intellectually they are often ahead of boys of the same age and this means that girls are more likely to be asking questions about donor conception. Emotionally, many boys and girls will probably be feeling the first stirrings of the hormonal changes heralding puberty. Parents may be noticing an increasing tendency by their children to seek the privacy of their own space and to challenge or answer back instead of co-operating as they may have done at eight or nine. Self-consciousness creeps in at this age and with it the beginnings of a reluctance to talk outside the family about anything that makes them feel remotely different from their friends, or inside the family about anything to do with sex. Boys seem to be the most sensitive to being 'different' over the pre-teen and early teens period. Girls are sometimes proud to flaunt their difference and perceive being donor conceived as 'special' in a very positive way.

Depending very much on your child's personality, temperament and how the subject has been handled in the family, donor conception may become a topic of great interest, with your child perhaps wanting contact with other donor conceived children (tends to be girls) or it may appear to be of no interest whatsoever (tends to be boys). Both of these extremes and anywhere in between is quite normal. Because of boys' particular sensitivity to being different from their mates, this can be a time when donor conception issues begin to go underground for a while, but this may not happen until puberty or at all.

Starting to 'tell' your child at 10 or 11 may or may not be tricky depending largely on how far down the path of pre-teen changes they are and how confident and prepared you are. Boys are most likely to still be more like children than teenagers at this age. The experience of three families in DC Network who all 'told' their sons at age 11, was that it went well and the families have all felt closer as a result. All three sets of parents sought support and guidance before 'telling' and found that this preparation was valuable in allowing them to practice language and feel as comfortable as it was possible to feel following 11 years of silence on the subject.

Following a Network meeting Jenny and Donald had been looking for an opportunity to start telling their son Jack age 11 about his beginnings –

> One evening the three of them were sitting in the lounge and Jenny showed Jack the book *Our Story*. She described it to him as, 'a book I bought to help you understand a little bit more about the treatments we received to enable you to be born.' Jack read through the book with his parents. He seemed quite content and did not ask any questions. Jenny commented later, 'We had anticipated the process would be very complicated, but as it happened all those years of anxiety seemed unnecessary.'
>
> Jenny and Donald had no idea how much Jack had understood as he continued not to ask questions, but before coming as a family to the Network meeting the following year Jenny asked him if he understood how his life had begun and would he describe it to her. Jack was able to explain in a way that made it very clear that he completely understood. On their return home from the meeting Donald was saying goodnight to Jack when Jack suddenly said, "Thank you for being my lovely Dad, I love you very much."

The guidance in the next section on Telling for the First Time regarding setting the scene, timing and language are likely to be helpful. You may also find it helpful to look at the booklet for parents of young people age 12 – 16.

'Telling' and Talking about Donor Conception with 8 – 11 year olds

Telling for the first time

Starting to 'tell' between 8 and 11 means choosing a time to sit down with your child to explain simply but clearly how they came to be conceived by donor conception and made you a family. Unless they are particularly young for their age or have developmental issues that make it appropriate for them to be treated as a younger child, their stage of development means that the gradual building block approach (useful for under sevens) is no longer appropriate. At this age children also really need to know the basics about sex and non-assisted reproduction before being told about donor conception.

You may want to think up and rehearse a 'script' for the time of first 'telling', or you may be more comfortable allowing the words to flow naturally on the day. Whichever way you choose to do it, remember that you are starting to tell a story that will be on-going.

We have included a draft script for you to base your first 'telling' on and also a suggested way for solo mums who have had embryo or double donation to add the information about using an egg as well as a sperm donor, something some single women find hard to do.

These guidelines have been put together following many discussions with donor conceived young people and their parents –

- **Offspring first** – put the emotional needs of your child first. It is the story of how they made you a family. The story of your infertility can come later. Share information with all your children (including those who came into your family other than by donor conception) either at the same time or within a very short space of time. If you have younger donor conceived children as well, you may want to start 'telling' them in a way that is appropriate for their age on a different day (see the booklet for parents of children aged 0-7).

- **Stage of development** – consider the implications of your child's stage of development. Put yourself in your child's shoes and ask yourself what they need from you. You are the person or people who know your child best.

- **Preparation** – think through what you want to say and why. If they are 10 or 11 include a clear but short explanation about why you have chosen to tell them now and not before. Don't be shy about talking it through with others such as a trusted friend, family member or professional counsellor – it may well help.

- **Support** – make sure there is someone in place that you can take your feelings to afterwards – here again it could be your partner, a friend you trust, a family member or a counsellor. Try not to burst into tears of relief or start telling your child how long you've been meaning to 'tell' them.

- **Timing** – choose a time when there are no other significant events going on in your child's life, such as tests for new schools, and make sure you have sufficient time after telling for any immediate response, questions and discussion. The start of the school summer holidays before you go

'Telling' and Talking about Donor Conception with 8 – 11 year olds

away can be a good time. Don't make an appointment to 'tell them something important'. Try instead to use a time when you would naturally be together.

- **Place** – home is better than a public place or a holiday resort. Your child may well need to be able to retreat to a familiar space of their own and/or contact a friend.

- **Language** – be direct in the way you explain about how they came to be part of the family. Give information clearly and simply and don't forget to speak with warmth about how much they were wanted and how loved they are. Too much detail about why you couldn't conceive is unnecessary. The older your child is the more embarrassed they are likely to be by the idea that you, their parents, might have had sex at all! The following is an example of how such a conversation could be started. It can be adapted as necessary for sperm, egg, embryo or double (egg and sperm) donation –

> "Dad and I have something we want to tell you about. Don't worry, nothing's wrong, but it is something important to do with how we became a family. Dad and I always wanted to be parents. Well, after trying for a while we discovered that it wasn't going to be possible to do that without some help. You know it takes a sperm and an egg coming together to make a baby, well sadly it turned out that my eggs were not up to the job, so with the help of (a clinic, hospital, doctor) we used an egg from another woman to help make you. I then carried you in my tummy until you were born. We couldn't believe how lucky we were to be successful in this treatment. When we knew I was pregnant we were thrilled and when you were born we were over the moon. We loved you then and haven't stopped loving you ever since. I imagine this might come as a bit of a surprise but we felt it was right that you knew before you got any older."

An example of how solo mums might add information about having used an egg as well as a sperm donor or embryo donation.

> "You know we have always talked about how I needed help from a sperm donor to have you, well now you are old enough to understand more, I wanted you to know that I wasn't able to use my own eggs either. The sperm and eggs that came together to make you both came from donors who wanted to be able to help people like me have a family. Of course you still grew in my tummy and I gave birth to you and we have been a family ever since."

- **One thing at a time** – give the basic information first and resist the temptation to heap more on them until they are ready. News like this takes time to sink in.

- **Acknowledge** how your child feels (or might be feeling) and show that you understand, without becoming defensive. Sentences beginning in the following ways can be helpful –

"I imagine that… (this might be feeling a bit strange for you)"
"You may be feeling… (a bit confused)"
"It would be very understandable…(if you had a funny mixture of feelings going round inside you about this etc.)"

- **Follow-up** – let your child know that this is a safe subject to talk about and that you are willing to discuss anything at a mutually convenient time. It is a good idea to initiate a discussion within a couple of weeks or so (and in the future) just to check how they are feeling and their readiness to talk but do this in a casual, matter of fact way.

In order to prepare yourself for your child's reactions and response to the information you are planning to give them, you may also want to think about the following.

Non-genetic parents and 'telling'

The parent who is not genetically connected may feel that they have most to lose from their child being told. Not only might they fear rejection, but some parents fear exposing their infertility, especially if they have avoided acknowledging it over the years. They may feel that it brings stigma and shame to them or their child.

These feelings are understandable, but they are not a reason for men or women to take a back seat when it comes to telling. Your children will need you and want you to talk with them. The experience of the vast majority of parents that DC Network knows of, who have talked with their children about their beginnings, is that rejection does not happen.

Genetic parents and 'telling'

It is not always the non-genetic parent who is most anxious about 'telling'. Sometimes the parent who is genetically connected has complicated feelings associated with fear of their partner being rejected or sometimes shame and stigma around using donor conception for family creation. Or there may be guilt about not having 'told' earlier and fear of a negative reaction from your child. If you are one of these parents, you may not even fully understand yourself why the thought of 'telling' feels so difficult.

It may well be that you have never spoken to anyone about how your family came into being or your feelings about this. Again, talking with someone you can trust could make all the difference.

Doing the 'telling' alone when you started parenting as a couple

In an ideal world both parents would share news with their child about how they came to be part of their family. But separation, divorce or death of your partner may mean that 'telling' alone is inevitable.

Whatever your situation, there seem to be two basic scenarios:
- *either* you have no option but to 'tell' alone because your partner has died or has been uncontactable for some time
- *or* the person you went into parenthood with remains in contact and therefore needs to be consulted or at least taken into account.

If you have to 'tell' alone, all the guidance offered here is relevant to you, but it is particularly important to take time to think through your own feelings first and find yourself some back-up. If your partner has died recently and you and your child are grieving, this is not a good time to 'tell'. Wait until you have both recovered sufficiently to be able to talk about your partner with love but without overwhelming emotion. It will be important for your child to know that he or she was much wanted by you both. You may be angry with your partner for dying and leaving you with the issue of donor conception (and everything else) to handle by yourself. It is helpful if you can acknowledge these feelings to yourself, but express them to a friend, family member or counsellor instead of to your child.

If you are *not* free to decide on and undertake the telling alone, again all the guidance here is relevant but this is a much trickier situation. Individual circumstances will vary enormously, but if the child concerned has a relationship, no matter how remote, with your ex-partner then this person has a right to be consulted or at the very least informed about your wish or intention to tell at this moment. All reasonable steps should be taken to involve and include the other parent in the preparation process, even if they are unwilling or unable to be present on the occasion of talking with their child. The reason for this is that the new information will almost certainly have an impact on the way your child thinks about or reacts to the absent or partially absent parent. If all attempts to reach an agreement with your ex-partner fail you may be facing acute dilemmas as a result of this dispute. If the courts become involved in this difference of opinion, a judge will assess what is in the best interests of your child – which, subject to appropriate timing, will mean that your child should be told the truth.

It is never right or helpful to tell a child about their origins by donor conception as a way of punishing or getting back at an estranged partner.

In the past some mothers have shared information about sperm donation with their child without letting the father know that this has happened. This is a strategy that comes with a high risk of accidental disclosure, as well as being an unfair burden for a child to carry. Where children feel resentment towards the parent who is unaware, it is unlikely that they will keep the secret for very long, leading to an unplanned confrontation that benefits no-one.

Support from good friends or family members, who can give time without needing their opinion to dominate, support organisations or a counsellor, is again highly recommended.

'Telling' if you have a known donor

Known donors are different to identifiable or 'willing to be known' donors in that they are already known to the potential recipients – couples or individuals – of the donated eggs, sperm or embryos. They may be family members, friends, acquaintances or, recruited via an introduction site on the internet. In the case of sperm donation, self-insemination outside of an HFEA licensed clinic may have been used for conception, or the couple or individual may have introduced their donor to such a clinic so that he could undergo the same testing procedures as other donors, thus bringing the insemination under the protection of the Human Fertilisation and Embryology (HFE) Act.

'Telling' and Talking about Donor Conception with 8 – 11 year olds

Self-insemination is only covered by the Act if partners are married or in a civil partnership. If insemination takes place this way and partners have not entered these legal states or a woman is single, then the donor will be the legal father of any child conceived. Single women and lesbians may be particularly vulnerable to changes of mind on the part of the donor. In recent years there have been a number of court cases resulting in donors being given similar access rights to a child as those that might be awarded to an estranged spouse or partner. A landmark ruling in February 2013 gave a known donor who had spent some time with the child he had helped conceive for a lesbian couple, was given the right to apply to the High Court for regular access to the child.

There are, therefore, many different situations and scenarios that encompass families who have chosen to use a known donor. This booklet is about 'telling' children about their beginnings, not about the choices that have been made by parents and donors prior to their birth. But some of these decisions have an impact on what and how a child is told about their conception. For instance, all concerned need to be clear about the nature of the relationship between the donor and the child. If the donor is a family member – and donation between two sisters or brothers is becoming more common – then it's important to be clear who is 'mum' or 'dad'. Donating siblings are 'uncle' or 'aunt' only and it is important that counselling prior to treatment has established that they do not consider themselves parents and all parties are confident they can keep their roles clear. The donors need to be sure they are not, for reasons of their own, needing to be recognised as the mother or father of the child conceived.

If roles and responsibilities are not clear in your family or you or your donor are struggling with how you feel about each other, or anything else to do with donation, it is vital for everyone's sake that you seek support and/or counselling. Your clinic may well be able to offer this service, but you can also seek independent counselling from one of the organisations listed at the end of the booklet.

Donation by a friend or acquaintance can also be a wonderful blessing or a potential nightmare. It all depends on the understanding of the parties involved and their willingness to keep on exploring together, with or without a counsellor, the long term issues – both emotional and practical – that are involved.

Under most circumstances, openness with children conceived with the help of a known donor not only benefits the child but strengthens the decision making of all the adults involved. Where there is honesty about what has happened there is no secret for anyone to keep or to be used in a manipulative way or as a bargaining tool. The only situation where openness may be more difficult to achieve is where a child is being brought up within a society, faith or culture that disapproves of donor conception. Parents in these situations face many challenges and have difficult decisions to make.

Beginning to share information with children between eight and 11 conceived with the help of a known donor is the same as for a child conceived with an anonymous or identifiable donor. All the guidance given in this booklet is relevant for this situation.

It used to be the case that most Network families with a known donor would explain about the basic facts of donor conception early but then share information about who the donor was at a later stage. This practice seems to have changed to most people bringing up their child or children with knowledge about and contact with the donor from an early age. This is likely to be particularly true when the donor comes from within the family or is a close friend.

Children accept donor information more easily before adolescence starts. This means that if you are starting to tell your child about their beginnings at this age, then including the identity of your donor is an essential part of what you need to be sharing with them either at the time of first 'telling' or as part of a follow up conversation soon after. You may want to use some of the language indicated in the section on Telling and add something like –

> "We wanted you to be able to know about the person who helped to make you so we chose your donor very carefully. Remember John, who stayed with us last year with his dog Sally…well he's the man who helped us to have you."

> "When we found out that we were going to need some help from another woman to help us have a baby, we wanted it to be someone who was as close to mum as possible so we asked Auntie Annie…and she said 'yes' so she's your donor."

No matter how very grateful you are to your donor, your child must be free to work out how they feel about this person for themselves, so it is sensible to go easy on the description of the donor as 'wonderful, kind, generous' etc.

If your donor is a family member or someone who visits regularly, then your child will almost certainly already have feelings about this person. They will need time to adjust to the new information and it will be important that they do not feel any pressure to develop a relationship that does not come about naturally.

> "Max age 11 has met his known egg donor, who is a good friend of his mother Ann. He was very good and polite at this meeting but his donor, who is awkward around children, probably because she is not yet a parent herself, did not really engage with him. She does not acknowledge Matthew's birthday and Matthew hesitated about putting her birthday in his calendar of family birthdays. Recently Matthew has said that he often thinks about his donor and that he is very grateful to her but has also said to Ann, "I am very glad I can grow up with you."

If you used a known sperm donor via a clinic or by self-insemination at home it is likely to be important to let your child know, one way or another, that you did not have sex with this person. Your child may or may not be curious about how the insemination took place, and if they ask you should be prepared to describe this process in as straightforward and matter of fact a way as possible. The older your child is the more embarrassed they may be about the process of producing the sperm. An eight year old may have technical curiosity that, on being told, could result in a similar exclamation to the son of a Network member whose story is told on page nine. A 10 or 11 year old may have similar curiosity but might not ask the question because of embarrassment. If they know the donor, they may be quite horrified that this man has performed such an act…something that they may be experimenting with themselves, but to a pre-adolescent seems a disgusting thing for an adult to do!

By contrast, egg donation is free from sexual overtones and the whole process may be one of intriguing fascination for this age group. Tim Appleton's adaptable books, *My Beginnings: A very special story*, which include some of the science of assisted reproduction, may be useful. But don't leave out the feelings either. All children being told for the first time of a genetic dis-connection and link with another person are likely to need time to adjust.

A known donor is likely to be someone that parents will want to keep up good (although not necessarily close) contact with until a child is old enough to make the decision themselves about what sort of relationship or contact they want. As in all human relationships, the keys to an on-going rapport between family and donor are respect, integrity and a willingness and ability to see situations from the point of view of the others involved. If all the adults involved can manage this, then there is great potential for the child to benefit.

Identifiable or anonymous donor

Anonymity for sperm, egg and embryo donors ended in the UK in April 2005 with a transition period until April 2006 when anonymous sperm and embryos donated prior to April 2005 could continue to be used. Since that time all UK donors have had to agree to be identifiable or 'willing to be known' to children conceived as a result of their gift once that young person has become 18. The same rules apply to sperm and eggs imported to the UK from abroad.

Most of you reading this booklet who have had donor fertility treatment in the UK will now have children who will be able to ask for identifiable details of their donor from age 18 onwards if they choose to do so. Some of you may (also) have a child who was conceived prior to the ending of anonymity so that your children have different rights of access to information (see section on Dealing with Difference).

Anonymity for donors was ended because of overwhelming evidence that it is in the interests of donor conceived people that they should be able to have information about the person who contributed to creating their life if they feel this is important and they choose to have it.

Many parents, however, have ambivalent feelings about children making connections with their donor and fear another person potentially disrupting family life and displacing the non-genetic parent in their child's affection. They feel that an anonymous donor would remove this risk. Sometimes for this reason and sometimes because of a perceived shortage of donated gametes in the UK, or for other reasons, many couples and single women have been and continue to seek donor fertility treatment, particularly egg donation, abroad.

Going abroad and 'telling'

Most of the countries that UK residents travel to for egg donation retain strict anonymity for donors. Some clinics in these countries give very little information at all about the donors. As a consequence some parents wonder whether 'telling' their child about their donor conception overseas is the right thing to do as curiosity about the donor would only lead to frustration. However, other parents believe that the imperative to be honest with their children remains strong and that learning later of a conception abroad might only add to the shock of late discovery. Many have decided that a policy of pride about the country and culture of the donor (and this may be different to the country in which the child was conceived) will help their child to feel a connection to the donor even if his or her details are not available. As comfort and confidence by parents about the decisions they have made have been identified as the most important factors in a child's adjustment to information about donor conception, this attitude is likely to help enormously. But it remains true that children conceived via anonymous donation abroad will find themselves in a very different position to children conceived in the UK at the same time.

We don't yet know how many donor conceived children, conceived abroad or in the UK since 2005 and 'told' in early childhood will want information about their donor. Informal and some formal research is showing that children 'told' early are likely to be much more comfortable about their origins than those who learn late, but curiosity of some sort is normal for them all.

Lessons from adoption

Although adoption is not the same as donor conception, experience from this field suggests that about half of adopted people seek information about their birth parents. A smaller percentage go on to meet their birth mother or siblings; more rarely contact is made with their birth father. Adopted women tend to search earlier than men. We can only speculate that an approximately similar percentage of donor conceived adults will want information about or contact with their donor. As donor conceived girls tend to ask questions earlier and more often than boys, it is likely that those conceived in the UK may seek contact with their donor sooner than will boys.

Whether conceived in the UK or abroad interest in and questions about their donor are part of a very normal process of identity building in teenage and young adult years. Young people often want as much information as you are able to give them in order to learn more about themselves and not because they want to displace, upset or hurt you in any way. Here again, the experience of most adopted people searching out their birth relatives is that the strength of their relationship with their adoptive parents remains intact throughout. In families formed by donor conception too, the emotional ties that have bound you together for so long are likely to be strong, unless there are particular reasons for them to have been weakened.

Telling when you have an anonymous donor

In the UK before 2005 all donors were anonymous, although there may have been significant non-identifiable information about them available. When the moment came, and on the whole children do not ask about their donor until they are 7 or 8, all parents had to explain that the sperm or eggs that helped make them came from a man or woman that they are unlikely ever to know. Parents sometimes added that they were sure this was a good person because they wanted to help another family have a child. As the rest of this booklet has indicated, if this information is shared in a matter of fact way then the child is likely to feel comfortable, at least until teenage years when further questions often arise.

Parents of children conceived abroad with gametes from anonymous donors can follow this model and add from time to time the information that they do have, including interest in and excitement about the donor's country of origin and anything connected to it, like places of interest, the weather, music or sporting achievements. A child may or may not choose to follow this up as they grow older but positive comments about the donor and anything connected to him or her are likely to help a child feel good about how s/he was conceived.

First and on-going reactions to being 'Told'

If your son or daughter is still more of a child than a pre-teenager then the chances are that any initial surprise or shock will pass reasonably quickly. Their response to the news about their beginnings is likely to be influenced by your preparedness and confidence, the circumstances under which they are told and your comfort in answering questions and being available when they need to talk. Initial reactions may vary from almost no outward sign at all to surprise and a need to ask many questions. Your assurance that they are very much loved will be important, but don't overdo it!

If your child is showing quite strong signs of entering puberty, and some girls in particular may do so from the age of nine or 10, then their reaction is harder to predict. A calm response may or may not hide a turbulence of feelings underneath. There could be some shock, disbelief and possibly anger. For children at this stage there may also be issues to do with why you have not given them this news before. "Can I believe you in the future? and "What else haven't you told me?" are typical anxieties that represent the loss of previously unquestioned trust in a parent. See the booklet for parents of young people age 12–16 for further information about 'telling' and teenagers.

Who am I?

The older your child is the more likely they are to be beginning to ask this question anyway as part of moving into teenage years. It is unlikely to be a conscious thought yet, but it may be reflected in behaviour such as wanting to be more private from the rest of the family. New information about their biological background adds another element to the quest for an identity that is uniquely theirs – "What have the genes I have inherited from my donor given me?" And as older children are increasingly preoccupied by their rapidly changing appearance – or watching for signs of change – it may well be physical likeness that becomes the focus of their questioning around identity.

The issue of physical likeness may well have already come up in your family, particularly if your child does not look anything like either you or other family members. Some donor conceived children and adults who do not fit in with the physical, intellectual or creative characteristics in their family have asked if they have been adopted or wondered privately if they were the result of an affair.

Issues of resemblance

The issue of resemblance between family members is often heightened in donor conception families. Although fully genetically connected children can be very different to their parents or siblings, significant differences in resemblance can be the cause of sadness and mixed feelings in both parents and children.

Sometimes children have colouring and features that are typical of the ethnic background of their donor.

> "Amanda and her partner went to Spain for egg donation. They were told by the clinic that their donor had blue eyes and light brown hair so that any child they had would fit into their family, which includes an older brother conceived without donor help. When their daughter Tamsin was born they were surprised to find that she had olive skin, brown hair and dark brown eyes. She is very beautiful but her difference to the rest of the family is obvious. Amanda and her partner found this difficult at first, particularly because they were on the receiving end of some very intrusive remarks. Now Tamsin is nine her friends are commenting about how different she looks from her mother. This difference makes Tamsin feel sad sometimes. She does not like being the only one in the family who looks different. Amanda feels that her daughter does not quite understand about the genetic dis-connect in the family yet as she has not asked questions about her donor. She anticipates doing quite a bit of supporting of Tamsin over the next few years."

Stephanie conceived both her children in the UK. Jessica age 13 was conceived with donated sperm and Sophie age 10 came into being with the help of a donated embryo.

Stephanie recognises the heightened awareness in her family, not just about looks but also temperament and personality. Both girls have Catholic sperm donors, one of whom is Irish, and Jessica has red hair, leading to much speculation about the Irish connection.

Jessica is a quiet and very self-contained person, rather like her (non-genetic) dad. She looks nothing like her genetically connected mum.

Sophie is a much larger person in every sense, taking up a lot of space in the household with her physical presence and big personality. In this she is rather like Stephanie, her non-genetically connected mum. Stephanie predicts fireworks from Sophie in adolescence, particularly when she starts thinking about her identity as an embryo donation conceived person.

Despite their differences the two girls get on well, although Jessica's patience is often tried! Stephanie says that not a day goes by that she does not think about donor conception in one way or another.

'Telling' and Talking about Donor Conception with 8 – 11 year olds

Keeping the lines of communication open, acknowledging feelings and offering appropriate opportunities for open discussion of these issues are likely to help.

Siblings

If your child has grown up with brothers and sisters, then they are likely to want to know if they too are donor conceived. They may or may not realise or ask about whether they share a donor and you will need to consider whether you want to volunteer this information immediately or keep it for another day. If your child asks directly, however, you should always answer honestly. This information may or may not be important for your children, but certainly some older donor conceived young people have found it to be a powerful revelation.

Caroline Lorbach recounts this story about an occasion when her son Andrew, one of their three sperm donor conceived children, was obviously trying to find out if things were equal in the family.

> "When he was about eight we were in the supermarket fruit and veg section. I was picking out tomatoes and Andrew was across the other side of the aisle looking at all the varieties of nuts. He said in a loud voice, 'I think I'm bright because of the man who gave us the sperm.' Well, what do you say to a statement like that?
> 'Maybe you're right,' I said.
> 'Did Dad have enough sperm for Callum?'
> 'No,' I answered.
> 'Did he have enough for Elizabeth?'
> 'No.'"

There are both advantages and disadvantages to a situation where siblings have been conceived by different donors or indeed only share one genetic parent for some other reason. If, for instance, one sibling wishes to search for their donor and/or half-siblings and the other does not, then it may be an advantage if they do not share a donor. But where both siblings wish for information, it may be more difficult if one is able to make a connection and the other is not. When siblings do share a donor it is important that different needs for information are taken into account and respected, although this may be tricky to manage practically.

Dealing with difference

Many Network parents have children who have come into the family in different ways – non-assisted conception, donor conception with different known or anonymous donors, through adoption or as step-children. You may be anxious about explaining the differences between them, particularly perhaps if some have access to information about genetic parents and others do not. Between eight and 11 children are capable of understanding about changed circumstances or new laws if shared in a simple and direct way. Tell them that you would not necessarily have planned the differences but that sometimes things turn out this way. It is also possible that a child conceived abroad will become aware as they grow older of the rights that UK donor conceived children have and ask about these. It is likely to be helpful to think about this in advance and have a simple explanation that is congruent with the facts and is not defensive in any way. Whatever the difference, the more matter of fact you are about it the more likely they are to accept it as one of the many differences between all human beings. But if your child is upset then the best response is to listen to and acknowledge their feelings rather than trying to brush them aside because they are uncomfortable for you. Reassure all your children that they are loved equally, even if they are sometimes treated differently because they all have their own needs. If the difference between your children is that one or more of them is connected to both parents genetically and another is donor conceived then the *Mixed Blessings* booklet, which can be downloaded as a pdf from the DCN Bookshop on the website, is likely to be of help.

As a parent it is easy to feel bad about not being able to provide everything your child wants. But don't beat yourself up. By being honest, listening, acknowledging feelings and generally being there for them you are doing everything you can to provide them with the tools (resilience, high self-esteem, self-awareness) to cope with what life throws at them.

Making genetic connections. Questions about the donor and half-siblings

Because of the development that has taken place in most children's brains by the time they are eight, questions about the donor around this age are very common. You may have shared some of the non-identifiable information you have when talking about looks, skills or talents in the family or you may be thinking about doing so. Following on from this, an understandable question that often stumps parents is "Why can't I meet him/her?" The answer will partly depend on the rules of the country in which conception took place, but you can always in the first instance say that the donor is someone you don't know but you do know that they are someone who wanted to help other people have a family to love. At six or seven this might be enough for most children but eight to eleven year olds may well want to know more. If you conceived in the UK then this is a good time to explain fully about how they will be able to get identifying information about the donor at age 18 if they want it. If you have not applied to the HFEA before now for information about any further non-identifying information about the donor they may hold (sometimes clinics do not give it all to recipients) then this may be the time to do it in consultation and collaboration with your child. You may also want to ask about half-siblings conceived with sperm or eggs from the same donor. As a parent you are entitled to know how many there are, their genders and years of birth. This is all information your son or daughter can ask for themselves when they are 16 and they may want to wait until then so it is important to talk with your child before applying to the HFEA.

Children are unlikely to spontaneously ask about half-siblings until they are at the upper end of the 8 - 11 age range and introducing the topic before puberty starts is a good plan. It can be a strange idea for a child – and often parents as well – to think about someone who shares something as fundamental as genes, growing up completely unknown in another family. Children may be fascinated with the idea or completely uninterested. This can change either way over time. In families where donor conception matters are on the everyday agenda then either of these responses or anything in between is completely normal. But children will pick up on your feelings about these things and if you are obviously uncomfortable with the topic then your children may feel that they cannot show an interest or ask questions. Many parents have quite complicated feelings about acknowledging the existence of half-siblings or indeed the donor as a real person. If this is true for you then contact with other parents via donor conception, a chat with someone in the DC Network office or a visit to a counsellor may help. Parents who are able to remain calm, confident and supportive, accepting that curiosity and interest in these links are a normal part of some children's wish to know more about themselves, are likely to be rewarded with a continued strong relationship.

If you conceived in a country where donors are anonymous then you will need to explain simply that the rules that applied at the time mean that it is unlikely that the donor will ever be known. You can talk about the sibling/donor registries that are developing as a way of linking people who are genetically connected but it is important to remember that they rely on the donor or half-sibs coming forward voluntarily.

Your child may be perfectly happy with the amount of information available or be very frustrated by it. Talk with them about the balance of nature and nurture (we are all a mixture of the two). Listen to them and let them know you understand their feelings, whatever they are.

The Donor Sibling Registry in the US is open to families from the UK (and indeed if you have used an American donor then this is THE place to make sibling connections). DC Network also has a registry called SibLink in the Members section of the website, where information about place of treatment and donor descriptions can be left with a view to allowing half-siblings to know each other before the age of 18 if that is what is wanted. DNA testing via companies like 23andme or FamilyTreeDNA is becoming more common and some donor conceived people have found genetic relatives, including their donor this way, but it does not inevitably lead to connections being made.

If you have a donor who is known to you then you will either have been sharing information about him/her with your child already or will need to make a decision about when to introduce this knowledge. See section on Telling if you have a Known Donor p15.

Many DCN families have found that if children have brothers or sisters, genetically or non-genetically connected, in the household in which they are being raised then there often seems to be less interest in half-sibs in other families, although curiosity about people who have genetic links is a very normal part of development. Our own daughter, now in her 30s, was brought up with two (half) brothers and consequently has no interest in male half-sibs, but a sister would be very different.

Talking with others

Family and friends

Telling your child about their beginnings by donor conception definitely means that *some* other people need to know as well. Every child deserves the support of their close family and adult friends of the family who are likely to be around as a child grows up. That said, those outside of this close circle do not necessarily need to know, unless it is for reasons that will benefit your child. Teachers and doctors, for instance, are likely to find the information of value in supporting your child and understanding any medical conditions they may have.

Because so many people find sharing information with others more challenging than 'telling' children, DCN has produced two booklets specifically on this topic. *Telling and Talking with Family and Friends* is for the donor conception family and *Our Family* is to give to relatives and friends to help them understand more about the thoughts and feelings of the family, as well as giving information about the law and regulations surrounding donor conception in the UK and how this might differ for conceptions abroad. There are also useful hints and tips on What to Say and What Not to Say! These books can be bought in hard copy or pdf from dcnetwork.org

Particularly if you are 'telling' for the first time at this age, you may be anxious that people outside the family should not know more of your business than they need to. You may want to be 'open' with your child, but also let them know that this is private family information. Although younger children would find it very confusing to be asked not to mention donor conception to others, children from around the age of eight are capable of understanding that there are some people and some settings in which it may be better not to mention it. This is because it would not be understood or because people just don't need to know. However, it is vital that you are honest with yourself about why you do not wish your child to talk with others. Is your concern for them or is it for you? It may be a mixture of the two. DC Network has always drawn a distinction between secrets and privacy. Big secrets are usually kept because at some level people feel ashamed or fearful. Privacy is what every family is entitled to. But if your child feels that they cannot mention donor conception to a friend without upsetting you, then you may have to think very hard about the kind of message that your child is getting about how they were conceived. Could it be one of shame or embarrassment? If so, you may want to think again and possibly talk things over with your partner (if you have one), a trusted friend or counsellor.

If your child has known about their beginnings for some time then it is probable that a selection of other people also know. These are likely to be close family and friends and those in your child's local support network, including perhaps the parents of your child's closest friends. You may also have shared the information with teachers at school so that they would be in a position to support your child if they choose to talk about donor conception in class (see the next section on school matters). Your family doctor is likely to already know your circumstances, but if your child has had to see another doctor, then you may well have 'told' this person when they asked about family medical history.

At some point from about the age of eight you will need to decide, with your child, when the information about donor conception should become theirs to share as they choose rather than yours to share in their interest.

> One Network dad came up against this issue when he told another parent in the playground, whilst they were waiting for their children, that his son (age eight) was donor conceived. He later mentioned this conversation to his son who was absolutely furious. "How could you?" he said, "And to Andrew's dad of all people." The dad thought about it for a bit and then thought, well yes, he's right and apologised to the boy. The time had come for it to be his information to share as and when he saw fit.

School matters

Children of around eight and nine are often very open and unselfconscious about personal matters. Some will choose to tell friends about donor conception or mention it if a related subject comes up in a lesson at school. In an early edition of *DC Network News* I told the story of the way our daughter, then aged nine, brought the topic up when the class teacher was talking about the shape and size of earlobes and how these are determined by genetics.

> Susannah said, "What about me, I'm a DC child." Her teacher, whom we had told about Susannah's beginnings, responded in a matter of fact way and asked her if she would like to tell the class about DC. She said she would and when she faltered a little, the teacher helped her out. They then returned to the lesson. We only learned about this episode a couple of days later when Susannah told us in a scathing tone about how stupid her friend Sophie was because she thought you could catch germs from being made by DC! Far from being upset by Sophie's remark, Susannah couldn't believe how ridiculous her classmate's comment was. Her confidence about being conceived this way meant that the remark did not press any 'hurt buttons' for her.

Some children are very frustrated that many of their friends do not understand when they try to explain about donor conception. The friends often seem to think that they must have been adopted. The use of donated eggs, sperm or embryos to help make a family is not yet on the curriculum of all schools for sex and relationship education so is not well understood, even by older children. As a result of comments about their experience in school made by a panel of young people at a DC Network conference, DCN is developing some materials for teachers, parents and young people to help widen understanding about donor conception in schools.

> "When Max got involved in a conversation with a friend about big families he tried to explain about his known egg donor and her family, but the friend could not understand and thought he was part of a step-family. He stopped talking about egg donation to friends after that as it was "Too difficult to explain."

Children in lone parent or lesbian mother families do sometimes have difficulties at school, but experience in the Network seems to show that it is the response from others about the perceived lack of a father rather than donor conception that is the root of the problem. Teasing and bullying at school around this issue can sometimes be an issue but intervention by teachers and parents working together to support a child can help. A teacher may be able to normalise the circumstances of a child with an innovative classroom project that brings up the issues but does not point a finger at the child concerned. If other children see the child's 'difference' being normalised by the teacher then they are much more likely to be accepting of the situation.

> "When Tom and Amelia were 8, Amelia told solo mum Lucia that a lot of the kids at school were asking where their daddy was, even though Amelia had tried to explain about donor conception to them. She was so upset that Lucia sought a meeting with the twins' teacher.
>
> The teacher already knew about Tom and Amelia being donor embryo conceived and was very supportive. The next day, during circle time, she read the whole

> class a book called 'And Tango makes Three' (based on a real story about two male penguins who adopt an egg and raise the chick when it hatches) in order to encourage the children to discuss issues of 'difference' in families. Lots of children responded, sharing the fact of their parent's divorce, being raised mainly by their grandma etc.. The teacher did not single out or mention Amelia or Tom who just said, "We don't have a daddy, we just have a mummy'. From that day on they have never had anyone from the class ask them about a daddy again."

Putting donor conception or solo parenthood into the context of the many differences that there are in how families come about or live their lives, can help normalise a child's situation and take them out of the spotlight.

An older child of a single parent decided that education about donor conception issues was what his classmates needed.

> Sandra, a single parent of three children, recounted in the DCN Journal how her then 11 year old son prepared, as part of his English homework, a three minute speech about donor insemination. She wrote, "He described the process of fertilisation and talked about infertile couples or women without men using donor insemination as a way of having children... He went on to the ethics and human rights of when does life begin and what should happen to frozen embryos. His final point was that he and children conceived by donor gametes should have the right to information about their donors.
>
> *Feedback from the class was good – he was voted the most interesting speech and he got a brilliant grade from his English teacher!"*

Another child of a solo mum brought up the subject of his conception when he went on a school trip to St. Paul's Cathedral. On seeing a statue of a Spanish saint he commented to one of the parent helpers that he and his sister had been conceived in Spain. The mother concerned already knew about his beginnings by embryo donation because the boy's mum was very open about it, but this occurrence is a good illustration of how children of eight or nine can demonstrate their understanding but also their confidence about mentioning donor conception when talking with other people.

For children in heterosexual couple families, it appears that far from being a cause of teasing or bullying, other children tend not to be interested – hence the frustration felt by children for whom the subject is of interest! If teasing does occur, children who have been brought up with the knowledge about their beginnings are mostly well able – like Susannah – to deal with it without too many problems.

> Katharine age 11 said, "I have attempted telling my friends about it but it has been quite difficult because they don't really grasp the idea. Two of my more intelligent friends managed to understand it and asked some intelligent questions. Most of my other friends said, 'So are you sort of adopted then or are you an orphan' and other really odd questions. So I sort of gave up with them and focused on telling more people who actually understood."

'Telling' and Talking about Donor Conception with 8 – 11 year olds

As sex education usually starts towards the end of primary school, it can be helpful for parents to check out exactly what is on the curriculum. If donor conception is not mentioned as one of the many ways to start a family, then a visit to the teacher concerned to ask for this to be added can be a helpful way of normalising the situation of donor conceived children.

> "Egg donor conceived Max is now in the top class in primary school and about to study sex education. With Max's permission, his mother Ann talked with the teacher about including donor conception as a way of normalising Max's situation but without pointing him out. The teacher was very responsive and asked Ann if she would like to come in to school to talk about it. Max was very happy for his mother to do this. Belgian culture is far less open than the UK about donor conception and Ann hopes that she is helping to open a door for the future by doing this."

Network members have mostly found teachers very open to being able to support children in this way. For many teachers these days families formed through donor conception are one of the less unusual family forms they come across. Hopefully the availability of materials for schools from DC Network will help teachers to feel more confident about including donor assisted conception as a normal part of teaching and talking around sex and relationship education and different ways of building a family.

One Network parent wrote:

> "When Sarah was ten I spoke to the life skills teacher at school when they were doing sex education to ensure that all artificial forms of conception were covered in lessons so that she would recognise herself in class discussions. I was careful to say to the teacher that there are now likely to be a number of children in any year group who have been conceived this way… or adopted etc. who will need to be OK about this; the teacher was very receptive.
>
> Sarah is now 11 and heavily into pre-adolescence; we are very aware that this is a difficult time for her in establishing herself with peers and feeling 'normal'. Because of this we are trying to respond to her needs and so donor conception has taken a back seat for a while, although I am keeping an eye on the sex education at her secondary school and will speak in confidence to teachers again if it seems right. We noticed in a work book from school that they had been talking about genes and had an exercise where they drew themselves and wrote against it from whom they had inherited what. She had written down several things she had inherited from her dad and sisters. What this means for her we are not sure but such pieces of work at school raise a number of questions."

Final thoughts

Deciding to tell your child or children how they came to make you a family may or may not have been a challenge for you. Whether this has been a straightforward or more difficult path, be reassured that 'telling' is undoubtedly easier in the long run! As a parent of two adults now in their early thirties, I cannot imagine what life would have been like during their childhood and teenage years if we had not had donor conception fair and square on the family agenda. Even though they are unlikely ever to be able to know anything about one half of their genetic backgrounds, they are both adamant that they feel respected as people for having been 'told': and they have a very loving relationship with their dad, their non-genetic parent.

If you Google 'donor conception' you may well have come across a number of websites that feature stories of donor conceived adults who are unhappy about their situation. Some feel that only identifiable donors should ever be used and others believe that donor conception is inevitably damaging to donor conceived people. It is sad and distressing to read these stories but important I think to acknowledge that they are there and that it is likely we have something to learn from them…mostly I think about the importance of being open and listening to our children.

A donor conceived adult in Belgium who is very active in talking about her situation posted a warning to grandparents on Facebook, saying that if their children became donors they would be giving away their grandchildren. Ann decided to test this notion with her egg donor conceived son Max. He thought for a while and then said that he certainly did not feel that he had been given away. He added, "If I had been conceived into that family (his donors) I wouldn't be me."

It should be noted that the donor conceived person who spoke about children being 'given away' had had a father who rejected his donor conceived children. This kind of dysfunctional upbringing is typical of a number of DC people in the UK and around the world who are unhappy about their beginnings, and/or their parent's deceit in not 'telling' them. Although not all come from backgrounds like this the vast majority were 'told' or found out very late about being donor conceived and mostly under very difficult circumstances.

There are of course no guarantees about how any of our children will feel as they grow and have thoughts of their own, but being raised in a loving and open family is likely to give them the resilience to manage difficult feelings should they arise in the future.

Official support for 'telling'

'Telling' and 'openness' are recognised as important for children not just by psychologists, social workers and counsellors, but by bodies such as the UK government, the Human Fertilisation and Embryology Authority, the Human Genetics Commission and the American Society of Reproductive Medicine. In contrast to a few years ago, very few UK doctors today would recommend secrecy. It might be easy to assume that such a high level change in attitude would make the task easier for parents. However, because this change is relatively recent and it remains such a personal area for a couple or individual, it may well be that many parents will still find themselves taking deep breaths before starting to talk with their children for a while yet. As in-vitro fertilisation (IVF) has become accepted as a very ordinary way to help with the conception of a child, so donor conception is well on its way to becoming part of public general knowledge as one of the many ways that a family can be created. Openness can only help.

Mixed feelings are OK

For parents there is a temptation to feel that once 'telling' is well under way, then your own feelings about donor conception are likely to settle down too. This is true for most of the time – 99 per cent of DC family life is the same mixture of everyday routine, fun, drama and drudgery found in any family – but just sometimes there can be a resurgence of the sadness and mixed feelings that were around right at the beginning…when you first realised that you could not have a child without the help of a donor…when you accepted that your child did not look like you or your loved partner. Don't worry or feel guilty about having these feelings. They certainly do not mean that you don't love the child or children you have. You may just be wondering what a child that was genetically connected to you would have been like and feeling sad again for a moment that this was not possible. It's very normal.

Remember that children develop in different ways

Throughout this booklet there has been a lot of information about the developmental stages your child is likely to go through between eight and 11 – from older child to pre-adolescent. But as each child develops at their own rate parents need to try and 'tune-in' to where their particular child is in their understanding and what is required from them as parents. One of the difficulties of doing this is that our own feelings have a tendency to get in the way. It can be helpful sometimes just to stand back for a moment and ask yourself, "OK, just what is my stuff here?" before responding to a question or comment from your child. Once initial 'telling' has been accomplished your responsibility is to bring up the subject from time to time just to check what they understand and whether they have any questions. Some children will need no prompting at all and others may appear totally disinterested. Both extremes and anywhere in between are completely normal.

Children appreciate it if both parents, genetic and non-genetic, mother and father (if a heterosexual couple) bring up the subject of donor conception. David, father to Dan age nine, was honest enough to admit that he rarely talked with his son about donor conception. He shared this story –

> "While enjoying the pleasures of family life, it is easy to forget about all the implications of having a child by donor conception, and go for long periods without mentioning it at all. 'You never talk to him about it,' Suzie my wife said to me one day. 'It's always me.' My immediate response was to deny this, but she was right of course. I made an effort and was rewarded with a new conversation with Dan. It is important for all of us that we keep the dialogue going."

'Telling' and Talking about Donor Conception with 8 – 11 year olds

It is important to remember that most of the challenges that may come up in the lives of you and your children are likely to have nothing whatsoever to do with donor conception! It is easy to jump to the conclusion that it may be the underlying reason for things like emotional or behaviour problems, developmental delays or difficulties at school. It is of course possible that donor conception (you or your child's response or attitude to it) may be a contributory factor, but the experience of Network families is that most times there are other explanations.

Final words from parents

One parent wrote about her experiences of 'telling' her now 11 year old daughter specifically for the How to Tell project and summed up her approach in the following way –

"We have tried to –
- always keep the fact that she is a donor conceived child in her consciousness through 'normal' conversation so that it never comes as a surprise to her in later life
- respond to her at the time and level she is at
- always be honest about what is possible/not possible and true and not true."

John posed and gave his answer to the following question at the end of an article he wrote for *DC Network News* –

> "So what responsibilities do we parents have towards our donor conceived children?
>
> Firstly, we have a responsibility to be open. Our children have a right to know that they are donor conceived.
>
> Secondly, we have a responsibility to listen. We must listen to our partners, if we have them, because neither parent will have all the answers and sometimes our partners have important things to say to us – things which we may not want to hear. We must also listen to our children because they are the ones who are most affected by our decision to have a family in this way and we must understand and respect their needs – needs which don't necessarily match our own. And we must listen to ourselves, for what we think we should feel about infertility and donor conception is not necessarily what we actually do feel about it, and it is important for us to recognise this.
>
> Thirdly, we have a responsibility to celebrate the genetic identity of our children. It is this last responsibility that has been brought sharply into focus by the lifting of anonymity for donors (from April 2005). It is perhaps the most challenging because it requires us to admit that our children are indeed different."

And that really sums everything up rather well. I hope this booklet has given you food for thought and confidence to continue talking with your children about their beginnings, which are now becoming just part of the complex story of who your children are and how your family is developing.

Further Reading

Some books, by their publication date, may appear to be rather old. They are included here because I am unaware of anything more contemporary that surpasses the knowledge and wisdom to be found within their covers. Most of the social and emotional issues around donor conception have remained the same for many years, despite the fertility world having changed significantly in so many other ways.

- Ken Daniels. *Building a family with the assistance of donor insemination* (Dunmore Press, Palmerston North, 2004) Available only from DC Network in the UK.

- Diane Ehrensaft. *Mommies, daddies, donors, surrogates: answering tough questions and building strong families* (The Guilford Press, New York London, 2005)

- Ellen Sarasohn Glazer *The long-awaited stork: a guide to parenting after infertility* (Jossey-Bass Publishers, San Francisco, 1998)

- Ellen Sarasohn Glazer and Evelina Weidman Sterling. *Having your baby through egg donation* (Second edition, Jessica Kingsley Publishers, London, 2013)

- Wendy Kramer and Naomi Cahn, J.D. *Finding our famiies: A first-of-its-kind book for donor conceived people and their families* (Penguin group, New York, 2013)

- Caroline Lorbach. *Experiences of Donor Conception: Parents, offspring and donors through the Years* (Jessica Kingsley Publishers, 2002)

- Olivia Montuschi. 'You're not my father anyway...' March 2005, in Personal Stories on the Donor Conception Network website: www.dcnetwork.org

- Mikki Morrissette. *Choosing single motherhood the thinking woman's guide* (Be-Mondo Publishing, Minneapolis, 2005)

For those who like ideas and research studies

- Petra Nordqvist and Carol Smart. *Relative Strangers: Family life, genes and donor conception* (Palgrave MacMillan Hampshire, 2014)

- Katherine Fine (editor). *Donor Conception for Life: Psychoanalytic Reflections on New Ways of Conceiving the Family* (Karnac London, 2015)

- Susan Golombok. *Modern Families: Parents and Children in New Family Forms* (Cambridge University Press, Cambridge, 2015)

- Michael E Lamb, University of Cambridge. *Mothers, Fathers, Families and Circumstances: Factors Affecting Children's Adjustment: Applied Developmental Science* 16.2,98-111, 2012

This article is a meta-analysis of very many studies about the many factors that affect children's adjustment. It includes and refers specifically to children in new family forms. Available to DCN members from the library of DC Network.

Parenting and child development

- Nicola Morgan. *Blame my brain: the amazing teenage brain revealed* (Walker Books, London, 2005)

- Andrea Clifford-Poston. *The secrets of successful parenting: understand what your child's behaviour is really telling you* (How to Books, Oxford, 2002)

- Adele Faber and Elaine Mazlish. *How to talk so kids will listen and listen so kids will talk* (Piccadilly Press, 2001) One of the best parenting books on the market

- Hollie Smith. *You and Your Tween: Managing the Years between 9 and 13* (Netmums, 2011)

Books to help explain about sex and reproduction

For parents
- Dr. Miriam Stoppard. *Questions children ask: and how to answer them* (Dorling Kindersley, London, 1997)

For parents and children
- Robie H. Harris. *Let's talk about sex: growing up, changing bodies, sex and sexual health* (Walker Books, London, 2005) Written for 10 to 14 year olds.

- Robie H. Harris. *Let's talk about where babies come from* (Walker Books, London, 2004) Written for 8 to 12 year olds.

Further Reading

Books to help explain about donor conception – for parents and children

Our Story

The Donor Conception Network has published a series of story books for young children about their origins in simple, positive language.

- *Children conceived by sperm, egg or double/embryo donation in heterosexual families* (3 books)
- *Children conceived by sperm donation in solo mum families*
- *Children conceived by sperm donation in lesbian parent families*
- *Children conceived by double/embryo donation in solo mum families* (customisable for twins etc...)
- *Children conceived by double/embryo donation in lesbian parent families* (customisable for twins etc...)

Archie Nolan: Family Detective, an illustrated story book for 8–12 year olds.
Open Archie's secret diary and join him and his friends on an action-packed adventure to find out what family really means.
(Donor Conception Network, 2015)

Telling and Talking with Friends and Family, One guide for parents helping them to explain to the wider community about how they conceived their children and one guide *(Our Family)* to give to relatives and friends to help them understand.
(Donor Conception Network, 2013)

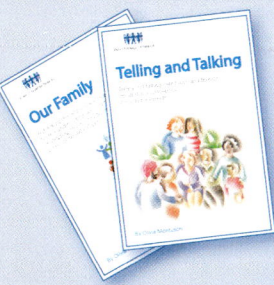

All these books are available from the online SHOP at dcnetwork.org

Other books

- Tim Appleton.
  My Beginnings: A very special story
  (IFC Resources Centre: available from www.mybeginnings.org)

This resource, which is available with a CD rom, can be adapted for many different assisted reproduction situations. It is aimed at the older child who may be more interested in the scientific and technical aspects of assisted reproduction and is especially valuable for children conceived via embryo donation, for whom there are few resources available.

- Jane T. Schnitter. *Let Me Explain*
  (Perspectives Press, Indianapolis, 1995)
  This American book for 7-11 year olds conceived by sperm donation into heterosexual couple families is sadly now out of print. DCN has copies available to members in the library. It is particularly suitable for girls.

Books about different sorts of families

- Todd Parr,
  The Family Book and *It's Okay to be Different*
  (Little, Brown Young Readers, 2010 and Little, Brown Young Readers, 2009)

- Cory Silverberg, *What makes a baby: a book for every kind of family and every kind of kid*
  (Zoball Press, 2015)
  Also available is an excellent *Reader's Guide* also by Cory Silverberg which we highly recommend.

- Mary Hoffman with Ros Asquith illustrator.
  Welcome to the Family; different ways a baby or child can come into a family
  (Frances Lincoln Publishers, 2014)

Films

A Different Story...Revisited DVD
(Donor Conception Network 2014)
Contains two films, one featuring children and young people from heterosexual couple families and the other from solo mum and lesbian families. All talk about their thoughts and feelings on being donor conceived.

Telling and Talking about Donor Conception DVD
(Donor Conception Network 2006)
Parents and children talk about their experiences of telling. Includes couples (heterosexual and lesbian) and solo mums.

Both films are available to buy from the online SHOP at dcnetwork.org

Archie Nolan: Family Detective
A funny illustrated story for 8-12yr olds

Science geek Archie Nolan tries to keep a low profile, but when his class are told to research their family tree, he is terrified twin sister and school swot Jemima is going to reveal that they are donor conceived. Archie's in turmoil. He doesn't want to talk about all that embarrassing stuff. The only person who understands is his donor conceived friend Cameron, but he seems to have unearthed a village vampire…. and Archie's far more interested in investigating that!

Open Archie's secret diary and join him and his friends on an action-packed adventure to find out what family really means.

This is a great resource for donor conception families, exploring themes of difference, friendship, connection and family. It's meant to be a conversation starter and is a great companion to this Telling and Talking booklet.

Available from our online shop
Please look on our website for more details about the book, who it's aimed at and what topics it covers.